through this journey,

you are still here

AMARI LANI

To my family and friends,

Thank you for pouring into me. Whether it was a tiny moment or one of the greatest accomplishments in my life, you've helped mold me into who I am today. Thank you for loving, teaching, and inspiring me.

Truth

They say the present is a gift
But so is time.
The turn of events sometimes
Alters your mind.
You probably wonder who's
Really there in the darkest times.

Life is short.
We may not always
Get a goodbye.
So have faith and trust
God will always provide.

The beginning isn't far
From the end.
Who will survive?

- It's funny how hello always ends with goodbye

- It's funny how good memories can make you cry

- It's funny how forever never really seems to last forever

- It's funny how friends leave when roads get rough

- It's funny how people change and feelings fade

- It's funny how one night we can regret so much

- It's funny how ironic life can turn out to be

- But, the funniest part of all is this: none of that's funny to me.

Just let that sink in.

Distracted.
Mind blown.
Approachable.
That's what this generation is filled with.
Young men who don't actually know how to...
Respect women, approach us like
We're humans.
Not like a piece of meat.
Tamper with us, and say things like...

Man, she's finer than me.
How do you expect me to...
Wanna even associate with you
When you approach us like...
Dogs,
Like we are less than you?
I wonder what happened to the old days.
You know,
When a guy would tell you...
"Hey, how are you doing today?"

Actually take some initiative
In this thing called approach.
Nowadays, when men approach women
It's awkward and makes us petrified.
Women.
Just play nice, smile
In hopes that will make them GO AWAY!
Sad thing is...
Women don't always get a break.
Men use their power over us.
Almost like pointing a knife to our throats.
Telling us we can't say no.
Nah.
That's not all men.
Just the ones who use this thing called
Approach.

it's so sad at such a young age
these kids are already messed up,
drinking their problems away
maybe, even
drowning out their deepest sorrows.

everybody wants their
cute 5 quick minutes of fame.
for what?
in this game, i refuse to play.

let's talk about ya morals…
giving up your respect
is basically telling yourself
to not to have respect.
for whom?
not just for yourself
but for the next.

the next pretty girl
who gets used and taunted
by a boy
who thinks power is respect.
listen.
you need to check

but instead, think.
about ya intellect.

how can you expect
anyone to respect you,
if you can't even
respect yourself?
we choose to lose our respect
and settle.
for what?
something that's less than us.

baby girl,
trust me
if he's the one
he'll have your respect

if you say no.
he won't beg.
he'll wait.
he'll listen to what you say.

see that's what's...
see that's
what's wrong with
this polluted generation.
we think
pressure is the answer
and sex clears cancer.

it's sad how I think...
about the next generation
after us.
Man

respect goes a long way
and it starts within yourself.
if you lose track, despite
who asks you next

please remember
respect is your covenant
and giving that up is
telling everyone around you
that...
you don't even
respect yourself.

In this day and age, we live in a world
Where everybody wants to be
Somebody.
You know the feeling...
Of being important.
Noticed.
Maybe, even wanted?

In this generation.
We look, search, and seek for...
This eight-letter word.
Called APPROVAL.
From our peers.
Seeking attention from someone
Just behind a screen?
Like, are you kidding me?

We look to hear the opinions
See the comments.
We feed into the
Fury.

The slandering disrespect
That we feed off each other.
The I'm sorry, but she didn't do THAT.
And the...
Who told him, he could EVER be that?

We believe so heavily...
That the opinions of others really matter.
When in reality, guess what?
THEY DON'T.

Throughout life.
We'll always
Look, seek, and search for
This eight-letter word:
APPROVAL.

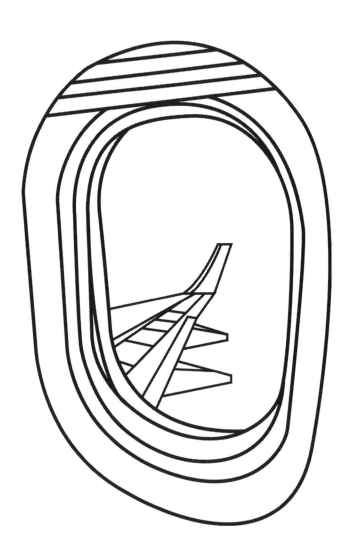

Truth is, you're scared.
Scared for the future.
Scared to grow up and make decisions.
On your own, for yourself.
It's like when you're a kid,
You're so ready to grow up,
But once you're grown up,
You're so ready to be a kid again.
I find that so ironic, how life works. Right?
I mean,
Life is all about choices:
The good, the bad, and the ugly.
But you're nervous.
Nervous, to move on.
Move away.
To go out and follow your dreams
That maybe aren't so practical.
Or even many would say predictable.
Of course, everyone wants a kid to grow up
And be a
Doctor, lawyer, nurse.

The list goes on. Really?
So they can have a...
Practical job, where they can make
At least a good salary. You know after taxes?
Maybe even work decent hours?
But would you be happy?
When you realize you no longer wanted to be this one thing?
You couldn't lie to yourself.
You just had no interest.
So until you discovered what you wanted to do,
When grownups would ask you,
"What's your plans after high school?"
You'd said, "Oh, you know, I don't really know."
You give a simple indirect answer:
"You know, I'll major in mass communications."
Maybe public relations?

Two waves crashing into each other. That's how it feels sometimes. You don't have to have everything figured out at 16, 17, 18 or even 19 years old. Trust me. My path isn't ordinary. I used to love thinking I was going to plan out my entire life. From when I got married, to when I was established in my career, to even when I was going to have kids. It was pretty fulfilling back then, I guess. But my path. My path isn't ordinary. It's solely experiences. See me, I'm an old soul. An eighteen-year-old girl who listens to old-school music, sometimes dresses like she's from the 90s, and wishes she grew up in the 80s. I'm just different. Like a rose that grew from the crack in the concrete, by Tupac Shakur. See? Like that.

Some days do you tend to feel...incomplete? At times, you just never really know what's going on. Maybe you felt this way all along. From your junior year in high school to freshman year of college, as if you just don't belong. In a daze, just wandering. You didn't know then, and you certainly don't know now. Unanswered questions that you're probably still asking yourself now: are you going back to school? Do you really want to move away? What are you trying to prove? Will it be worth the experience? I'm here to say that you are still SO incredibly young. Your path may or may not be ordinary. But remember, you are never too early, and you're never too late.

You cannot question why things might've happened this way or that way. Sometimes, things just happen. It doesn't get any simpler than that. You just have to trust that everything will get better. I think it's time for you to be completely honest with yourself. Maybe you don't want to go back to school. Or maybe it's just not the priority right now. Don't make any decisions if it feels forced. Forced to be put back inside. Inside this box, to do and to be "practical." And believe me, there's nothing wrong with practicality.

If there's one thing I've learned about me, a practical girl just doesn't live inside me. I've never been the girl to do the "right thing" or to take the easy way out. My heart lives inside my dreams. It's time to face the facts. This is me: my good, my bad, my now, my past. Simply, just me. Incomplete.

dreams.
that's where I have to go.
go to get away from this.
imagination free world.

a life where I cannot dream.
have goals and aspirations.
just because it's not the right way
doesn't mean it's not the right way.
for me.

please, let me go.
don't hold me back.
I am on a mission.
just a girl, with a plan
and a vision.

life may not go as we planned it,
but I refuse to go into my battle.
blind to the sight of where I'm supposed to be.
no, being practical doesn't mean I will or
will not succeed.
life is about following my dreams.

I am sick.
sick and tired
of hearing negative comments and opinions.
"oh, you'll never go back"
and
"you won't make any money doing that"

no, forget that.
who are you to tell me what I will be?
everyone's purpose in life is different.
different choices, different outcomes.
life will always be
about the journey, never the destination.

I know how hard this must be for you. But right now, at this very moment, I need you to let go. Let go of every single person who hurt you. Every person you hurt. Every time you felt broken and didn't know why. To feel that every single thing that you touched you already damaged. I need you to forgive yourself. For not allowing people into your world. Because every person who entered your life, you became close to them and they somehow always leave. It's not your fault, trust me. Some people are just good at one thing and that's leaving. Some people just forget about you. Almost as if you never mattered to them in the first place. You don't trust people because all they do is hurt you. You're so afraid to let someone in and actually love you. Because you're afraid they'll break you. You're so fragile. Just precious cargo. Cargo that gets easily attached to every owner. And at the end of the song, they'll go pack you away. As if you were a travel bag being stored only to be used for the next leisure of adventure. But in order for you to grow; I really need you to let go. Let go of every situation that is out of your control. Every person you searched for love in. Every person who broke you. Every person who lied to you. Every person who ignored you. Every person who just gave up on you. With no explanation why.

Remember that feeling where they took your heart out from your chest and left you with absolutely nothing. Each and every time your heart was in the operating room being fixed on, you left your heart bare and exposed. On your sleeve. In the hands of those who left it shattered. It had to be sewed back together again. Every little tiny rip and crack that was in it never truly healed. Your heart was just rearranged. Every person you would open up to only destroyed it more. Left it a little more weak and brittle than it was before. Stop searching for the love you owe yourself inside of someone else. Don't give them the power to hurt you any longer. Just be happy with you. Stop disrespecting and allowing yourself to settle for a situation. A situation from someone you'll never hear from again. From someone who simply just doesn't care about you. It's a new season coming in your life, and its name is uncomfortable. Learn the love you need to give yourself. Understand that this pain that you feel in your heart doesn't last forever. Just be clear and honest with your intentions.

Surrender.

Pain

You don't know how you should feel
Some days you're happy
Lately you've been sad
Maybe not sad like you're depressed
Maybe just stressed and tired
Like you're losing everyone around you
Maybe you're losing your mind
You're not insane, but are you really sane?
What happen to the person
Who had the most beautiful sun
The one who was supposed
to brighten others day
The one with "happy" feelings
But strikethrough the happy
Part. You know why? Because how can
You be happy in a world that's so cold.
Full of destruction and sadness
That makes you sad. In spite of all this
You miss your friends. Some who have been there
Since you were young,
Before high school.
I bet you wonder if they hate you now.
For what?
Maybe leaving them, maybe moving on.
Apparently...
You're not the only one who's moved on
As you replay constant old conversations
In your head. Your heart is begging to say
YES. but
Your head says no.
It's like, one day they love you.
Then the next they don't.
How could they be so blind?
How could you feel so stupid?
Maybe, you THOUGHT they were different.
As your conscience screamed to you
"Sweetheart, this isn't a movie. This is your reality."
Some people will never love you the way you love them.

It's crazy how the people you love the most...
Can somehow still disappoint you.
Make you feel less than.
As if your feelings don't matter.
When THEY make the choices THEY make.

Ever since the day they left
You have waited.
Waited for the day
You could say they finally saw you.
You made it.

It's been so long.
Somehow, you forgot how they look.
But their voice sounds just the same.
Just age.
Man. You couldn't think of
The last time you saw them...
You just remember being so happy.

Time finally caught up.
Now your heart feels empty.
When you realize they won't be there for you.
All you could think is...
How?
How could they do this to you?

Now every time
They get in contact with you,
You ignore them,
Because why would you believe them?
You believed in them. Never judged them.
I guess that's how it feels when you know...
They won't change.

You say you want the best for them.
But they have to want
The best for themselves
Too.

Empty.
Not even sad.
Really, just numb.
A heart that is lost and incomplete.
A tornado with a sign of caution
Labeled "destruction inside."

An endless cycle of those
Hurt people, hurting people,
Pretending to be okay
For everyone else who's around.
Family.
Friends.

When people turn their problems into yours
You become immune to them.
Almost like the flu.
And I'm sure it's been like this for a while.
You just didn't notice.

So yes, things came off the wall.
But being trapped inside a house
And not a home is even worse.
Trying to act like everything is okay.

A constant image replays in the back of your mind
As you walk around pretending and acting like it didn't.
You felt helpless.
Gasping for air.
Screaming stop.
Who heard?
No one.

Trauma makes you look at life a little bit differently.
It makes you feel affected.
That every time you see things
It's a reminder of your pain.

Of trying to cope with the negativity.
To clean your heart.
Forgive those who hurt you.
Apologize to those who you've hurt.
No one should be unhappy.
Faking it and smiling like
They are happy.

"I know your secret"
Maybe. They've matched or attached you to...
a name.
See I don't do too good with the...
"match the name to a face" but maybe
It's more like "match the face to the story I've heard"
Or wait I got it.
How about we
match the boys and girls to their messed-up ways
Any person despite how they appear are kings and queens.
The darker the berry the sweeter the juice,
But imagine for young black men and women to hear,
"Oh, you're cute for a dark-skinned person"
"Man, you got dark"
Do not break my brothers and sisters melanin down
Because you hate yourself.
You hate your people.
I am not you.

Maybe I'm not even your people.
Let me tell you this, though: I love my people.

Honestly, when you're a different shade out of the crayon box,
you think....
you don't have to worry about these same issues, right?
No, you're wrong.
Being black is a choice yet at the same time a
PRIVILEGE.
The same black culture that gets acquired and used
Each and every single day

Being ignorant does not give you the right to
talk about people of the same or different race as you.
Degrade them because of their skin color.
A lot of people don't know what it feels like to
be asked these questions.
So, they remain ignorant.

These things come in waves. Group A. Group B. Group C. It's just at different times, with many turns. Almost as if this thing we call life is... a rollercoaster. A lot of highs, but there's so many dirty lows. Our bodies. We carry these stories. They're called scars. It doesn't have to be physically. It could be mental. Every time you lay inside a bed, flashbacks. Flashbacks of things you wish to not remember. Things that haunt you every time you close your eyes. That's why you choose not to blink. To protect. Protect your eyes from the craziness that you live in. That someone can give up on you because you're not what they wanted. That they can have the audacity to still leave because you're not the only thing they see. Hearts broken and bruised. Your heart cries when you realize that people don't care about you the same way you do. But yes, everything is easier said than done, right? WRONG. It's hard to give up on someone you gave so much to remember. It's hard for your heart to say yes when your mind says no. It's hard for you to just walk away when they're all you know and want. Some people just don't know the damage they can really do. And it's not even just their words, but their actions too. When they stop caring, it's like a little piece of your heart dies when that person leaves. Your heart hurts because they left nothing for you to remember them...

Bye.

You break us down and judge us.
You say things like…
Man.
She's a 7 in the face.
But definitely a 10 in the…
Want to only see us, unclothed.
For your journey.
Newsflash, we're not airplanes.
No, you do not get to take a ride
On our mystic journey.
Don't get me wrong, all women want to
Feel good about themselves.
No matter; size, color, height.
But we refuse
To let you use us up, as your own sexual pawn.

Excuse me,
But do you actually see nothing wrong?
I mean, come on.
It's a new decade, and we're still fighting for…
Hello? The BIG picture?
Our RIGHTS.

You know there's something I just don't get…
When a man does something,
9 times out of 10 it's justified.
Once we do it, it's like KEEP rolling.
Are you getting this???
Like no, this chick did not just say this.
We get taunted.
Abused, with the words that roll off your tongue.
Kicked and bruised up
Hearing the tone of your voice.
Every name that we get called.
What do you think that does to us?
WOMEN.

Would you dare...
Call the woman who gave you your life this?
Now, I know what people will say:
Didn't we go half on a baby?
Yes.
But who has to carry a life
Inside of them for 9 months?
WOMEN.

Slander.
How am I supposed to build a home
If you're taking my bricks?
This isn't just about men against women.
Yet more, women against women.
Just because we don't like the same things
Doesn't mean we BOTH can't be it.
STILL.
We are constantly breaking each other down.
Like that girl really thinks she's the whole kit.
Self-esteem.
Confidence.
WOMEN.

Women DESERVE their voice.
We don't just belong in the kitchen
Or having and taking care of the kids.
We can HAVE dreams too, you know?
At the end of the day.
No matter who tries to kill your dreams.
YOU. ARE. GOOD. ENOUGH.
WOMEN.

Heat of the moment. Soft sun kisses braced over your neck, leaving noticeable purple-reddish love bites. Then it leads into something a little more. Now there's a tongue pressed against your sacred area. Young women taught to "save ourselves" for marriage. What about our young men, though? The ones who carry Magnums inside their pockets and flaunt it, trying to label themselves "experienced." The guys who pressure girls into having sex with them. The ones who pretend like they're truly interested, when it's really just a silly game to them to get inside her pants. If not, he'll just move onto the next. Women being labeled and having to place a big red "A" on their chest like Hester, demonstrating their scarlet letter. Their shame. Tattooed on permanently to define whether she's good in bed or not. These young men and women are obviously confused. We're so afraid of being able, we settle for something that we're not comfortable to do. Instead of waiting for someone to find us, we search and desire to be in a "relationship" and end up in a "situationship." That alone is not what you're good for. You are so much more than just a fun time or an exhilarating high. I get you might want to have fun, but for only one night you get what you wanted, then what? You two may never speak again. How do you think that makes the other one feel? Tainted? Used? Abused?

All because you were faded. All in one night, so many regrets can occur. Think about the trauma created when that young girl or boy puts their head on their pillow at night. Broken and bruised. Crying because no one can fix the damage that has been used. Being emotionally damaged is not natural for anyone. We twiddled our thumbs at the well-known apps like stupid Tinder to hook up. What happened to getting to know each other? How can you be comfortable being with a bunch of people you don't really know? There's something that you have to deal with inside and you cannot hide. A void you're trying to fill. Women. We are not wired to just have sex with multiple people and think our feelings won't be involved. We're the receivers in the process. Something is being penetrated into us. We deal with the pain that comes along with having sex, not the man. While, men are the givers. Most times, they're just trying to get a quick touch. That's why they say things like: "It didn't mean anything, I was only trying to not do too much." Not thinking about the bed full of mistakes. Insecurities. No room for acceptance. The anticipation. The walls caving full of "first times" The sad thing is when the awkward conversation comes, we begin to compare and sometimes it's not even. It's just one too many. The harsh truth and reality. That maybe she's just not good enough. Maybe he's not good enough. If you can't talk about it after, maybe you shouldn't be doing it in the first place. The harsh and sad reality we call sex and intimacy.

Letting Go

time doesn't measure up.

remember the girl, who had a smile
as bright as the sun?
remember the girl, who listened.
who cried.
who carried so much hurt?

remember her voice?
her lips.
her heart.
she loved.
but guess what?
it wasn't enough
for her.
so she gave up and walked away.

she waited.
for so long.
years.
to at least, try.
try to have a relationship
now she's left to pick
her broken heart up.

now, it's time to
let it go
there's no point in
holding on.
when she's given,
all she can.

she said, "loving someone isn't easy."
and it's not supposed to be.
but she also said:
"trying to be with them, shouldn't be...
this hard."

and for her.
she realized.
she loved.
to the moon and back.
she would do anything.
to cherish this just a little longer
but at this very moment.
she's done.
she's tired.

she can no longer wait.
because waiting, is like.
waiting for the sun to tell the moon
"I love you."

To all the people you never planned on losing: it sucked, but thank you. Thank them for the journey. For the experience. For being a part of your life. I bet you never would've imagined meeting someone like that too. It all just came in like a flood. Just constant rain for days. Months. From sunny August to sweet, crisp, cool November. You just crashed. Doesn't it suck to feel sad about someone? And not sad about them for a week, and you move on. Sad for when you think about them all night long. For like weeks, months, years. It's the weirdest thing. You wake up and they're on your mind. You could be happy and suddenly somewhere you're reminded of them. You see their name, their page. Just something that draws you back to them every freaking time.

But what's the point of feeling sad about someone who doesn't even think about you? You sit back and really think: "Oh how, I miss the person you used to be." The person who was in love with me. Who went above and beyond to show how much you mean to me. Someone to tell you how beautiful you were. How fearless you seemed. But now. Now you've learned, I deserve better. For now. I choose me. Now you no longer wonder what they're doing. Or do you miss me? When they gave up on you. That's when you learned you needed to let them go. In order for you to breathe. Your scars will heal, it just takes time. Day by day you'll find your way. You learn that every decision you made wasn't a mistake. It was a choice you chose to make. So yes, you're allowed to miss the person they used to be. But you're better off alone and happy than unhappy and alone with... them.

you're my ...

- could've been

- should've been

- would've been

but never was, and never will be.

True colors began to shine only with time. I guess that's why they say third time's a charm. Apart of you only hoped the rain proved her wrong. But little did she know he's just like the rest. Just another name added to the list of people "she can no longer trust." She never asked the rain to pour. She was the sunshine in the midst of his melancholy. The golden light that fills the hearts of not only the rain but so many others. And maybe for the rain. That's what HIS problem was. The rain couldn't handle the fact that the sun shined for everyone.

Rain was bitter and destructive. The sun began to wonder why time after time the rain would create thunder. She never asked him to wait. Because why wait for something that may never happen? The sun NEVER got mad when the rain would shower on the clouds. But the rain was ALWAYS mad when the sun warmed the other clouds. They were total opposites, never equal. Almost like night and day, just two totally different moods. Now, the sun doesn't know. And she certainly doesn't care. She was a good person and I guess the rain never realized that.

Or maybe he did realize that, but he couldn't settle to be less than something to her. All the rain ever thought about was himself. And the sun realized she couldn't hold on to what the rain used to be. She forgave him and moved past it. But sometimes, people aren't like the memories we know them to be. Some people change just like the seasons do.

This is the last year of settling for less than what you deserve.
This is the last year of you being financially unstable.
This is the last year for feeling small
when you're around others.
This is the last year of you being unemployed.
This is the last year of you hurting from
people who are no longer in your life.
This is the last year of holding too tightly to things.
This is the last year of you not stepping
out on faith and just trusting God.
This is the last year of not chasing your passion.
This is the last year of you crying over
someone who doesn't feel the same way.
This is the last year of feeling like you are not good enough.
This is the last year of feeling overwhelmed
with people you can't change.
This is the last year of falling short of your dreams and goals.
This is the last year of putting everyone
first and making yourself second.
This is the last year of trying to control everyone but you.
This is the last year of silencing your tongue and
being afraid of other people's judgment.
This is the last year of searching for
closure everywhere except in you.
This is the last year of wanting someone to
give you love in order to feel loved.

This is the last year of making a big deal out of little things.
This is the last year of you saying you can't, when you can.
This is the last year of waiting for something to happen.
This is the last year of "trying to make things work."
This is the last year of living in fear
for being who you truly are.
This is the last year of choosing everyone, but yourself.
This is the last year of doubting who
you are and your self-worth.
This is the last year of being the same person with no change.
This is the last year of you giving up on what you truly love.

Maybe. He's just her imagination. Maybe he's just a tainted and faded memory. Maybe. She hoped and prayed that their story would've ended differently. With a plot twist, they both lived happily ever after. THE END. Or maybe she's just trying to convince herself that she doesn't miss him. But deep down inside, she knows, she always will. She searches for his voice in every song, his heart in every text message. Even his undeniable smirk in every photo. Crazy how someone could bring out the best parts of you while still examining and knowing the worst. He was someone who knew all her faults and never let them define her. She hated the fact that their paths might've crossed at the wrong time. That they never had a fair chance for their story. Before things even started, somehow it all ended. She felt like quicksand, stable at first but quickly sliding. That one mistake could possibly ruin their so called "forever." She hated that when they first met, things were so different... Before the person he's become. NOW.

He was always the first person she wanted to tell good news too. And the last person she wanted to ever disappoint. He was the only person she ever got close enough to hurt. She hates that she let him go. But the timing just never worked out. It was always when he liked her, she didn't like him. And then it went, when she liked him, he didn't really like her. It sucks because he's always on her mind. But he's probably already moving on to someone new. Possibly searching for her in every other girl. Someone who can be everything she never was. Despite his faults, she never thought less of him. And now, she's staring into a mirror, hoping and praying his reflection doesn't show up soon. He truly brought out the worst sides of her. But he also knew the best parts that never touched the light. He knew deep down his heart would always love her. Sad to say, they never made it to their happily ever after. They were bound by a permanent tattoo labeled strangers. And for them both, that might've been their deepest regret. In so many ways, she just couldn't explain it. But each and every day, she still craved him more. He became the person she buried away when he walked away.

Love

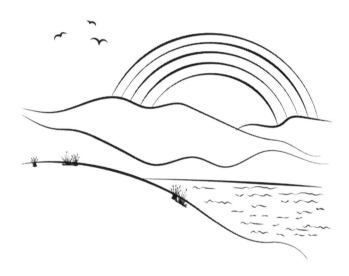

Dear whoever may need to hear this,

No one is perfect. Things might not have worked out the way you expected. Or maybe even how you planned it. I get it, disappointment sucks. But that's okay. That doesn't mean go jumping to conclusions, or say your life is over. The crazy thing about life is that it takes us all around in a full circle to get us where we're supposed to go. It's all part of a process. A process where we have to sacrifice doing the things we want to do for the things we have to do. Understand, this is just the beginning for you, my friend. You are so much more than you probably thought you'd ever be. You have a purpose that is beyond what your greatest dreams may be. Remember that you are so freaking special. Please know that. You deserve every star in the sky. Someone who loves you for you. You may not know it yet, but you have a gift. Maybe there's someone out there who needs to hear your story. There might be someone going through the exact same thing. So keep in mind. You. Are. Not. Alone. Yes, it may hurt today, but it won't be this way forever. Trust that, this is not the end. You are worth so much more. Learn to make mistakes, create personal experiences, and grow from testimonies. You are a walking miracle, a story worth telling.

PS, it's not over.

I miss the girl I used to be. The girl who always spoke her mind. Who wasn't afraid to say how she felt. A girl who never sugarcoated anything. She was brutally honest. Someone who sang at the top of her lungs and danced around like she was crazy inside stores. Despite it all. She didn't care what anybody else thought. With her, there was never a dull moment.

God places people in our lives at certain times. You know why. To show us that we need to have people around. These people who see things in us that we never saw in ourselves before. That even when it becomes difficult for us to realize, they remind us of a person we once were. To show us the qualities inside of ourselves that we hide away from the world. Hidden in a place for no one to see.

That girl that I once was has vanished. Some days, I reminisce. I begin to find that girl... I find her in every song I sing. Every picture I take. Every story I write. At times, I miss this girl because of who she was. She was so fearless. She never thought twice about things. Once her mind was made up, that was it. She was just a girl who lived in the moment and recognized that the present is a gift.

A girl who was so sure within herself. Crazy, because this is the same girl who still lives inside me. Every minute, every hour, and every day. Now, she's just buried into the deepest parts of me. The parts that are unseen by the light. There are still parts that do shine through. They show me that... she's wiser than she thought she'd ever be. This girl called things exactly how they are supposed to be. She's a boss. A beauty. A queen. This young woman is a force to be reckoned with.

This girl knew exactly who she was. Even when she was lost and confused. In a daze and walking through a maze with no way out. Wandering to find her purpose, her dream, her gift. She hopes to find her way, someday. Find what's meant for her. She knows things take time. That life is a feeling process. She's right where she belongs. The girl is slowly finding her way; she's a caterpillar turning into a beautiful butterfly. Through her ups and downs, a cycle of constantly trying and failing. But this one. She's picking herself back up, slowly but surely. One step at a time. Fearfully. Gracefully. Magically. Spiritually. She's simply at peace. The source of her own beautiful happiness.

I pray you find peace.
I pray you find strength.
I pray you find beauty in simplicity.
I pray if you're lost, that you'll find your way.
I pray your heart no longer feels heavy.
I pray you allow yourself to fall in love.
I pray you let people in to love you.
I pray you prosper in each and everything you do.
I pray you figure out the steps you need to take.
I pray you win in all your endeavors.
I pray you are happy.
I pray your family/friends are happy for you.
I pray you open your heart to new things.
I pray you bring positivity around your aura.
I pray you grow in this season.
I pray you find all the answers you're searching for.
I pray you find happiness within yourself.
I pray you find everything you want/need.
I pray you fulfill all the goals you make.
I pray you learn from all your mistakes.
I pray you find true love.
I pray you find your purpose.
I pray you have a phenomenal support system.
I pray great things are coming for you.
I pray this is your year.

Be selfish.

Sometimes.
Do you feel like you're fighting?
Against myself.
Heart in one hand.
Mind in the other.

Just to make it...
To make this so-called dream
Come true.

I just wanna make you proud.
I hope you say,
"Oh, look at you!"

I just want you to know
I always did it for you.
But now,
I know more than anybody.
I do it for me.
All the heartache and stress.
Long nights, where nobody knew.
I was crying.
Days where I would wonder.
Go to sleep at night, thinking,
Is it even worth it to you?
Everything you instilled in me.
I cannot thank you enough for that.
When I was down, you wiped my back.
If I could do it all again, would I?
No doubt, because through it all,
I could do it stronger.
Just to make the journey, it was worth it twice again.
So thank you.

I look around and think,
Wow,
All at my age. God blessed me.
Gave me goals.
Allowed me to have ambition.
And blessed with charm and charisma.

How many people can say they have that?

So if you have a dream, and if people
Don't want to see you make it,
Do me a favor.
Sit back
And make THAT dream a reality.
Don't ever look back.

Remember I told you THAT.

Dream It.
Live It.
Believe It.
And It'll Come to Be.

L-O-V-E
4-letter word.
Love is something you do
not because you have to.
We do not live on the same planet.
You are from Earth,
And my soul lives on Mars.
I am a great warrior, a prime believer in love.
Love is not you, nor I.
Love is not just how you act.
But what you think, what you say.
Love cannot be control
Love is its own dimension
How can you or I commit
When neither of us knows the base of love?
None of us are "unemotional"
So if you do not believe in the same love I believe in,
Does that make you any different from me?

Let's talk about history.
My ancestors.
Gods and goddesses of love.
Smooth, silky, sweet agape love.
Slavery did, and still does exist.
That doesn't mean we can't coexist.
Till this day, we are still fighting for our rights
Just to be here despite all the hate we get.
They kept us in the fields, tied up in bondage.
Crazy how it's the 21st century, and equality still isn't right.
Not just between you and me.

To my young black men:
You are kings.
Do not let society break you down.
To say you are less than.
That you'll just be another number
In this sick, twisted system
Have goals and aspirations.

You'll achieve them one day

Cover and protect our young queens.
The world will need you someday.
Even if they don't know it yet.
Become that doctor, lawyer,
Maybe even an NBA star.
No dream is too big.
Some may even tell you
It's too small.
Shoot for the moon.
You just might hit the stars.

Never let anyone tell you no.
Pull your pants up.
Hold your head up high.
Let them know
Black excellence can
And
WILL be achieved.

To one of the closest people to me,

How did I end up with you in my life? It's only been two years, and it feels like a lifetime. You are my... lifeline. My backbone. God knew exactly what he was doing when he placed you in my life. Your love is so unconditional, even when I'm being so hard-headed and stubborn. You tell me all the things I need to hear. You're someone I can count on. You truly love me for me. And when I am with you, everything in the world makes sense. Things that I never saw myself being able to do, I now see so clearly. You help push me to do better. To be better. To know I can have someone around me; someone I can be silly with who doesn't judge me. Someone who laughs with me when I'm singing at the top of my lungs, acting dumb. You've helped me not be afraid of what everybody else thinks. You've loved me the way I thought no one else ever could.

We can sit and talk about nothing for hours. The greatest thing is, we'll just drive around or walk for miles. Even when it's honestly nothing to do, it always feels like something with you. Now that you're away at school, I know sometimes we may not talk every day. And that's okay, but when we do, it's as if time never left. Never would I have imagined missing you as much as I do. With you being 164 miles away, a three-and-a-half-hour drive, it SUCKS. I just want you to know I am so proud of the young man you're becoming. I support you 110% with everything you do. I am so glad you're still able to do what you love beyond high school. You've made me a better person. A better friend. When we first met, I never thought we would be as close as we are now. And every time I re-read the letters you've written to me; I know more than ever that you saw things in me that I never saw within myself. I think fate really brought us together. To teach us a lesson that speaks volumes in ways that's so beyond who we are. Honestly, I never expected you to be my best friend. I didn't know what to do or where to start.

A best friend to me is someone who makes the bad days better. A person you call to tell all your boy problems to even when they don't want to hear them. Someone who just gets you. FYI, you're always the first one I call. You might've thought I was just another pretty face at first, but you got to know the real me. And if there's one thing you've always told me, it's to never settle for less. And with having you as my best friend, there's no way I'm ever doing that. Because of who you are, I've learned this is how it feels to be loved and valued. You love me more than life itself. And I know without a doubt you genuinely want to see me win. Words cannot explain how thankful I am to have you in my life. If you ever need me, always know I am just a phone call away. Even when you hardly ever answer my calls, I'll always answer yours. When they see you, they see me. I'll go through the ends of the earth and back for you. I got you forever. It's war over you. You already know that. And I promise no one could ever take your place. You know the real me. I cannot ever repay you for taking the time to get to know me for just being there for me. Thank you for teaching me what it's like to have a best friend. To feel loved. To feel that even when you're at a low, you're not alone.

Love always,
Your best friend xoxo

Dear future daughter,

You are so loved; even before I get to meet you. You are more than enough. You are my strength (in) heaven. I hope you're never afraid to talk to me about anything. You're so smart and vibrant. Remember your name as if it struck from lighting. I will be there to pick fights every now and then. I'm only doing it because I love you. And once you get older, I'm pretty sure I'll get on your nerves. (Always) But I'll also be there to push you. You'll never have to go through anything in life alone. You are brave and fearless. Wonderful and kind. You are allowed to be anything you want to be in this world. Remember, it's YOUR life. You set the path for yourself to be a doctor, filmmaker, scientist, or maybe even a writer. Black. Girl. Magic. Never take no for an answer, and always speak your mind. You were meant to be something. Something that's beyond just who you are. You have a purpose to fulfill in this life. Don't be wasted potential. I will always be on your team, cheering you on. I want you to be the leader and a fighter. When you win, I win. Your fight is my fight. Prepare me. You will become my greatest blessing and everything I never was. I pray you learn from my mistakes. I made them so you can learn and never have to go through what I went through. I just want the best for you. My light. My world. My heart. My future daughter.

You are beyond your years.
You are worth loving.
You are more than enough.
You are God's gift.
You are talented.
You are a ball of fire.
You are wanted.
You are a dream.
You are a fighter.
You are a prize.
You are a giver.

You are a source of light.
You are better than you were before.
You are gifted in various shapes and forms.
You are an ounce of sunshine.
You are going to be okay.
You are special.

You are all kings, queens, princes, princesses.
You are important.
You are enough.
You are loved.
You are a daughter, son, mother, brother, aunt, father, cousin.
You are fearfully and wonderfully made.

Most importantly,
You are a work of art.

About the Author

Amari Lani, also known as Zari Dakari, is a young adult author and poet. She lives in Atlanta, GA, and began writing during her sophomore year of high school. She graduated from high school and college at the age of 17 with an Associate Degree in Photography. For as long as she can remember, she's always dabbled with her creative side. She has always done things to express herself, whether taking pictures, playing the violin, making videos with her sister, or writing and singing songs - she is a creative. Whatever she puts her mind to, she accomplishes.

When Amari began writing, it was an outlet. It was a way to release as she dealt with challenging situations in her life. She felt understood being able to transfer her words into a safe place. Amari writes to be able to not only share her own personal experiences, but to have people feel and relate through her stories. At first, it started by writing about a lot of heartbreak and disappointment she went through. Then Amari realized she didn't want to write about her pain alone. She wanted to write about so much more. Amari Lani knew her purpose was to influence and empower young creative individuals, to use her voice to speak life into people and to inspire the world around her. So with each story she writes, there is always a message contained inside—a message that allows people to feel understood and to be able to grow from their experiences.

Her writer name, Amari Lani, came about originally as an anonymous name. She wanted to be able to express herself and share stories with the world on social media. The whole idea in fact was that she wanted to gain a following from people outside of those who already knew her. From the moment she realized she wanted an alias name, it was very crucial that the name carried meaning and significance to her. She wanted a name that symbolizes what she believes while still being a part of who she is. The first name, Amari, is based on her second middle name Mariama. Taking the first part, Mari and coming up with something that spoke volumes, her mom helped her come up with Amari, meaning strength. As for the last name, she wanted it to be memorable. She began looking at the different last names within her family. Then she thought about a name that stuck with her. She said if she ever had a daughter, she would name her Lani, meaning heaven. Thus, the brave fearless woman Amari Lani was born.

Made in the USA
Columbia, SC
13 July 2020